A

Oliver Reynolds was born i
drama at the University of H
Residence at the universities
Glasgow. He now lives in L
Albert Hall.

OLIVER REYNOLDS

Almost

faber and faber

First published in 1999
by Faber and Faber Limited
3 Queen Square London WC1N 3AU

Photoset by Wilmaset Ltd, Wirral
Printed in England by The Guernsey Press Company Limited

A CIP record for this book
is available from the British Library

ISBN 0-571-19747-7

Some of these poems first appeared in *London Magazine, Modern Painters,
New Writing 7, Planet, Poetry Wales, The Times Literary Supplement*
and *Thumbscrew*

2 4 6 8 10 9 7 5 3 1

Contents

Palinode

What is myth is not you.
What I wrote was untrue.
Men died for a decoy –
Your double sailed to Troy.

Greek

A headland. Heat. A single tree
drawn by the wind like a catapult
never to be released.

Then the sea's furnace-shimmer
heaves up this: the messenger
with his ingots of speech.

Throughout the rigmarole
of monsters and maidens
the commander unrolls maps.

The messenger is imperturbable
as an arrow. He is his mouth.
His wrecked body weighs no more

than an echo. Words
engorge his tongue
till he stops. Dead. Dumb.

Well

I went down, again, into myself,
as though down a well-shaft, dry
in the dry season, twisting down
an unseen rope of introspection
toward the deep sump of the self
and an all-cancelling dark broke
over me, ebb-tides of nightfall
clamming the eyes, ears and nose
till I descended by touch alone,
rough stonework curving round me
like an upended tunnel or a womb
or tomb or some passage between,
a cumbersome span of life built
from awkward blocks into water's
opposite, into a stone sentence,
a tower of thirst. My knees gave
and I stood, ankle-deep in dust.
I looked up. According to legend
the well, like a sunk telescope,
could throw a beam of blackness
onto the sky, turning daylight
to starlight. All I saw, though,
was a disc of unseeing, a blank.
Like Cyclops, dying, his one eye
its own obol, everything I saw
was nothing: this bone-meal moon
small and meaningless as an o.

The Calling

What might have been a whisper
faint as the gas-fire's pucker
or an intimation
like the first slants of rain —

was it the self
getting a whiff
of the noumenal
or a mind-mistral

sprung out of nowhere
to sigh in my ear?
'Acquiesce. Accept. Above all,
fail. Do your best and fail.'

What sounds like an echo
is wind at this attic window.
Drenched in particulars,
the world looks less

than itself — all these views
when I wanted a voice
as abstracted as air:
skittish, astringent, clear.

Instead, an unmistakable shape
is stamped on the clouds: a ship.
Above the roofs, bright through the rain,
a ship beats up from Kensal Green.

Doldrums of brick collapse and spill.
London's a sea. Crowding on sail,
the ship rides level with my eyes,
the name on her bows seized with ice:

HMS *Indifferent*.
A woman stands on deck, white as frost.
What could be thawing ice
is the sound of her voice

whispering, shy as snow-fall:
'Here is your work: to fail.
Here is your life: small rooms
and the mouse-scratch of small poems.

Here is your choice: no choice.'
The window shatters in a spray of ice
as the ship swings in, huge and sheer,
and a rope-ladder unfurls in the air.

The Usual

(a)

Except in memory
where, still, aloof,
he baits (or shares) our love,

poor Tom's his obit –

the force of a life
no longer alive,
a he no longer a he

but an it.

(b)

Son of a Jones
so some wisps
of the old tongue
clung to his:
wool on barbed wire.

(c)

Whites-of-the-eye swell
above the rim's tilt.

His glass gavels wood.
'Duw, I needed that!'

(ch)

Set on the parapet
    of his forearms
the stare is massive, load-bearing,
    like the bridge piles

he stares at, drunk, drinking
    in the river's
foam and physic
    all day:

how does
    what water
know to go
    which way?

(d)

A drinker
on a wall
in the rain –

the weather
inside worse
than that out.

(dd)

What we have, we have once.
As though in remembrance, pillow and bed
    Preserve the shallow dunts
Hollowed by a thin man: hip, shoulder, head.
    What we have, we have once.

[7]

Was this him
always moving east, as money does,

leaving a dawn coastline surprised
by a seal's quizzical head

and the annual tide turning
the drovers' trails white?

Or that sniffer of capital air,
wind hungover with hops on a brew-day,

which of the names of this drinking-man
known in The Old A and The Greyhound

was his, half-heard in the taproom din –
Tom or Thoms, Tommy or Thomas (Tommo to some)?

Was he any of these? Or none?
Or Legion, living on the lump?

This must be him, pioner of the M4,
tunneller, curser in a crash-hat,

thin as his shovel and as hard-edged,
the mouth on him diplomatic as a drop-forge.

And if pressed by a ganger or worse
(a desk-wallah dipping an avid nib),

he'd unearth one final name
and flourish it like a passport:

'Me, butt? I'm Jones. Got it? Jones.'

(f)

Hiraeth? Only once. At Smithfield.
When an artic's air-brakes
made him turn as they hissed and squealed:
a stampede of raw steaks

covered the road, their bummaree
unbalanced by fatigue
and the legend on the lorry:
HOPKINS. CARDIGAN. CIG.

(ff)

Shouldering his way through the meat-men
to order his brown breakfast:
'That's right, butt. The usual.'

(g)

How does
   what water
know to go
   which way?

An Englishman's Home

The house where we live is Salisbury Plain
and the guns go off again and again.

The kitchen's rather Maida Vale:
butler and governess, capon and quail.

The staircase here is Becher's Brook,
but climb it we must, by hook or by crook.

There's the bathroom, all Virginia Water.
The mad laughter's my mad daughter.

The master bedroom or Slough of Despond.
And the wife, bless her. She will not respond.

The Builders

Hefting hodfuls of air,
we have walled ourselves up.

Echoes walk the bare homes
built stanza by stanza.

Brandenburg Variations

You are Schadow, the sculptor, sketching your 'Quadriga', a four-horse chariot driven by a woman.

You are the informant (not to be named for reasons of national security) stealing an X-ray.

You are Euainetos, the die-engraver, coining it.

You are Ulrike Jury, naked and holding out a staff. You will be Peace on the city's western gate. Hoppla!

You are Ulrike's uncle casting her in copper.

You are the King. Cover her up.

You are Napoleon entering the city in triumph.

You are Houblon packing the 'Quadriga' into twelve cases for transit to the Louvre.

You are Blücher entering Paris in triumph.

You are Schinkel, artist and architect. Turn Peace into Victory: replace the Roman eagle on top of the staff with a Prussian one; add the Iron Cross.

You are a widow. Your boy runs down the street.

You are Cato the Elder. Carthage must be destroyed. You are holding up a ripe fig, asking the senators when they think it was picked. It was picked the day before yesterday. In Carthage. So close is the enemy to our walls!

You are Hannibal (with elephants).

You are Hess in the trenches, shot through the chest.

You are Control bidding. A quadriga and Nike by Euainetos, dolphins in the exergue (Syracuse). A palm-tree and horse-head (Carthage).

You are a Hohenzollern walking through the central arch reserved for members of your family.

You are H leaning over the model of Germania, your face hidden, your parting straight as the North-South axis.

You are the informant. You will exchange the X-ray for Lots 115 and 118. (You began your collection with a tetradrachm taken from a museum in Paris. Walking the bright boulevards, you quoted Cato.)

Your name is not recorded. You are the usher at the Opéra who showed round the Germans. H tried to tip you twice and was twice refused. The reason is not recorded.

You are Doctor Thomas holding up an X-ray. No scar tissue on the lungs.

You are not Hess.

You are Dönitz planting a tree which will be higher than the prison when you leave.

You are Dido digging, unearthing the skull of a horse. This is where the Phoenicians will found their New City.

You are Little Hanif running down a street in Tunis, running through marble and sand, through rivers of ash, a gate, your father's arms, an open door.

You are Fritz mixing mortar.

You are Kirsh, a guard. You are loading your rifle.

You are Marietta Jirkowski. You are eighteen years old and three months pregnant. For ever.

You are a decoy, a dupe, an eidolon.

You are Mitch from Hoboken. Bombs away.

You are the Goebbels boy playing in the bunker. Misch, Misch, du bist ein Fisch!

You are Speer walking the Great Wall of China in the prison garden. In your head, you are free.

You are Hermann Kempinsky opening a letter from the Todt Organisation.

You are Hannah, a hotel maid, bringing tea to two gentlemen. One examines a brooch by the window overlooking the Gate, the other holds a large brown envelope. There is no tip.

You are Meier recreating the 'Quadriga' from plaster casts found in the west of the city.

You are Schültz of Planning. No handover ceremony.

You are Heller checking your sector through binoculars at dawn. A cart and horses going nowhere.

You are Sharkov holding a hacksaw. Lose the eagle and cross.

You are von Schirach at the end of your twenty-year sentence. They return your effects, including an alarm-clock. You wind it up. It ticks, then rings. Deutsche Technologie.

You are Hans driving a bus through the Gate, whistling.

You are the last of the four to be unharnessed. The guards say your muttering keeps them awake. Heh, heh. Heh.

Wishes? These three.
The past's untrue.
You are not you.
And I'm not me.

What Was Said

The words you used then – winter
    blessing our path
with hesitant, considerate snow –
    are forgotten

now as I walk streets white
    with blossom-fall
and the swirly couplings of butterflies,
    but what was said

remains, and is revisited,
    memory thawed
to a feeling, an old path
    freshly revealed.

One More Time

You once swam with dolphins.
Now it's my swimming head
that holds and buoys you up,
girl that I call my boy,

or is it you floating
free, in your element —
being loved, knowing it —
anywhere, like water?

I call you lovely boy
and my beautiful girl.
Endearments. Confusions.
You are loved and unknown

so I name you — Adam
blinking at God's creatures
dumbly blinking at him,
teeming and tamed with words.

You turn, kick, in your sleep.
Your dreams are drowning you.
Commitment. Betrayal.
Your arms are wide and dead —

a sailor's last embrace.
My warrior. My girl.
I hold you by the feet,
fingers closed on each heel's

spire of bone. My soldier,
my Achilles, let me
lift you from the water.
Shivering. Immortal.

*

Towed by dolphins, you smiled
your dolphin smile, Venus
in a wet-suit, laughter
lapping your shining face.

Whose eyes were brightest?
Woman and dolphin talked,
sleekly sharing a joke
as ancient as Adam.

When I asked what you'd said
you answered with a burst
of dolphin-chatter, squeaks,
a shoal of syllables.

Their working-lives over,
the dolphins were set free —
a salt manumission
for they kept returning,

the pull of the harbour
deeper than any sea.
Our tidal years return
under the circling moon.

Held in my arms, you say
you are flotsam. How close
can we hold love and doubt?
Always this two-in-one—

our ocean-depths of doubt,
our rock-like certainties.
Each is, is each other,
foundering and founded.

*

You'll wake to my fingers
whispering in your hair,
spiralling your short hair
into a memory—

we are years ago now,
a boy and girl in bed,
my hand clutching the plait
towing me into sleep.

Years ago and today
the past flows into now.
We are the same river
flowing in a circle

and we are the sages—
once bitten, twice bitten—
gaily stepping in it,
each splashed footfall fatal.

If there is a last word
to our old argument,
our sweet contradiction,
it's left to the body.

We lie with each other,
our duplicitous tongues
dumbstruck, our wet faces
gilded by candlelight.

What we do is ancient
and shining with newness,
a first sunrise greeting
alps of air undersea.

Song

Like uxorious ivy squeezing oak,
   Green muscle grown moony,
I want you – now, before I croak –
   To hold me, just hold me.

On the slopes of sleep, let your mouth feed mine
   Till I'm replete
And in a dream both mortal and divine
   Heartbeat echoes heartbeat

While the panic of my pulse, calmed by yours,
   Slows into bliss
And seconds are rechristened hours
   By the ghost of a kiss.

Grant me this wish and I'll swear by your eyes
   I'm stuck on you
Longer than amber enamouring flies:
   We're mutual, we're two.

Submission leaves me smiling and fulfilled –
   No doubt, I dote –
The two of us will reach the Elysian fields
   In the one boat.

There – posthumous, mythical – we'll take in the view:
   The arcaded myrtles above
And the frieze-like lovers doomed to renew
   That old, old story – love.

Sometimes we'll dance where the river couched in its lair
    Plays a slow serenade,
Sometimes we'll rest in the harmonic air
    Of a laurel's deep shade,

Watching the random breeze rustle the leaves,
    Zesty with spring,
Of the orange-groves and the lemon-groves—
    Kingdoms where scent is King.

It's always April here, this girl who hugs
    Her green skirts to herself,
And mother earth's always naked here, her brown dugs
    Dribbling with health.

Then a clamour of welcome – the lovers of old
    Waving sprays of myrtle
Are walking our way – we're to be enrolled
    In the ranks of the immortal.

They sit us by flowers trembling with bees
    Encumbered by their yield
And each rivalled lover agrees
    We hold the field:

Whether it's Europa whom Zeus, cloven and horned,
    Carried off out to sea
Or Daphne whom the gods, to spite Apollo, turned
    Into a tree;

Whether Dido and Artemesia, the sad pair
    Who grieved their way to fame,
Or that fatal Greek whose beauty you share
    Just like her name.

14s for Helen

You are French. You're fourteen with long red hair.
   As we make love
On a Louis Quatorze chair, all you wear
   Is one black glove

And a silver chain singing at your neck,
   Jingling sunlight and air
As we sway to Putney on the top deck:
   'Deux allers à *L'Homme Vert.*'

Les Champs Élysées is the Fulham Road.
   Our bus fills with the crack
Of myrtle branches on the roof, their fragrant load
   Of incense and arrack.

We've brought Valentine's Day to November.
   London's asphalt orchard
Reflowers again as I remember
   My name for you: Orchid.

Mme de Maintenon, the past is now,
   Blaze and ember
As indivisible as Camembert and cow,
   January and December.

Quand vous serez bien vielle, I'll still call.
   My collar furred with snow,
My stick canoodling with yours in the hall,
   I'll be ardent if slow.

We'll take tea, then each other, by the hour.
    You are the pliant girl
I keep in la Rue de la Tombe Issoire
    (Every swine has his pearl).

The bus snorts, shudders, stops dead in its tracks.
    Looking down, we could swear
As the sun dapples us with dots and flecks
    The road is a river.

Our conductor speaks: 'It's not the Thames or the Seine
    Or the light playing tricks.
Look at it now, and then never again.
    It's the Styx.

Here's your change.' He puts pennies on our eyes.
    It starts to rain.
'Plus ça change...' is French for 'Surprise, surprise.'
    I blink, in vain.

Blubbing like kids, all the passengers stand.
    We remove our berets.
Tears sprout on our cheeks – cataracts of sand,
    Tell-tale berries.

You're English. You're my age. Your hair is brown and short.
    I take your hand.
After rain and river, blindness and sight,
    We reach dry land.

I am drenched with memory. Time and place
    Are this night,
This bed and the smell of tea-tree oil on your face.
    You turn off the light.

Silver charms whisper – your Star of David
  And your lucky turtle.
Then whiffs of heaven ... I must have drifted ...
  Eucalyptus ... Myrtle.

Caveat

Lovers are often blind
And poets lie on oath:
You're in a double bind
Trusting those who are both.

Elegiacs, Almost

I

Free of the bogies' beat and the train's rhythmical trample,
    Something else can be heard: musical, eerie, a sound
Moving like a shape, a billowing between the carriages
    Caught, suspended in air, just as gladness or grief
Step from a church into wind and every veil's astonished:
    Ghosts of the life ahead, ghosts of the life left behind.

II

Souls are not often granted to trains, but this wailing
    Could be a soul's last gasp, this random and wistful blues
Howled and whistled by a small-hours conjunction of metals
    (London Bridge fallen away, TV masts dotting the dark)
Could be a soul set on oblivion ... or just oblivion...
    Lethe babbling forever down to the sorrowful South!

III

But what it is, now, is memory: the mind's endless shuttle
    Fated to trek forever, fated to never arrive.
This train, though, is slowing and houses circle the station,
    One of them yours: Deptford's a synonym for home.
Searching for your window has become a ritual of arrival:
    Homecoming swears by sight, sight is the vows of the eye.

IV

There! You're in: that second-floor porthole, eternal roundel
  Lit forever by love – love, or a 100-watt bulb!
Deep in your accounts, jiggling your foot to the jagged rhythms
  Concentration keeps up, this is your absolute self:
Calculating ... a cigarette ... a sip of Balvennie ...
  Lion-golds in your throat, tawny one, talk to me now.

V

Tell me what happened that day I arrived in the summer,
  Sunlight prowling your bed, heavy and thick as a mane:
Tell me how light fell as heat and how we had to follow –
  Nothing between us then but a shimmering of sweat,
Tell me how you paused above me, stopping mid-kill,
    startled ...
  Tell me how you resumed: keener, keening as we came.

VI

Mirrored in the dead TV, you'd seen us, small and golden ...
  Somewhere, lives are alight, perfect as flames in the eye.
Keep them there, now and always, brighter for being smaller:
  Statues ambushed by tears, truth on a page that is blank.
Somewhere, drive-in cinemas are drifting into winter.
  Keep them, memory, for now: held, as we were held, then.

The Almost

I had a gift which I didn't give you—
Rembrandt's *Elephant* extending his flirty trunk
like a trombonist, a glad-hander or a drunk
with a brolly. Who we are is what we do.
This benign clown hauling a favoured prop
from the scuffed grey suitcase of himself
is all elephant; this life left on the shelf
is me; and you ... You are where the metaphors stop.
You are you. My gift went ungiven on a day
of waste, of feeling all but unwanted
from the moment I woke and heard you say
'I forgot you were here.' So solidly planted
at the centre of ourselves, is it the self we betray
or each other – gifts not given, lives not granted?

Lugubrious troopers, tail-to-trunk, trunk-to-tail,
on pillared legs, like bridges walking,
the pachyderms of memory sail
into view, unbudgeably huge, baulking
at nothing. That morning, I remember,
I checked my watch – your gift to me – and saw
it had stopped. Time whitened into permanent December.
Half-asleep when you left, I heard you lock the door.
Rogue omens clashed their tusks. What did they mean?
That farewell forgetting – did you want me
not there at all, or there for good? Come clean –
what am I to you? I slept. A key dreamily
resolved each lock and clock, each clenched machine
of the self. It was cool in your palm. Ivory.

Your palm. Your hand. My face nuzzles your hand
and your fingers tighten: my mouth quenched by your palm
or your fingers drinking my face? Wellings-up. Balm.
The solitary cloud above arid land
with its promise, its blessing of water.
You wear your mother's wedding-ring with a plain band
annulling it. Your palm is boundless, a dream land
where the weather is knowledge: your daughter
has her mother's hands. She lifts them above her head,
blameless, blessing and blessed. She is a babe in arms—
in your perfect arms; she is sixteen; she is dead.
Farewell was a final touching of palms,
then our one child was christened by a thief.
He took our girl and he christened her: Grief.

Grief-greys lost in white-out: elephants move
across tundra into the true north of the mind.
Blizzards of self. White lies as love
winters out; the thinned air it leaves behind.
The animals approach a secret death,
their pensive tracks obscured by pensive snow.
Farewell is the cold blossoming of breath
in this graveyard where the forgotten go,
the hurt, the harmed, the outcast from the herd.
The two of us turn in our sleep. A ghost
turns with us, the sleepless ghost of a third.
The might-have-been. The all-but. The almost.
Our bedside candle is the wavering doubt
lovemaking left us too tired to blow out.

A cigarette on the shores of the Med —
you're weighing up the sea, all but undressed,
paddling, smoking and, mostly, unimpressed.
An Amazon's arms and a big cat's head —
flat-of-the-sword muscle and the slow-lidded blink
of puma or panther. You take my breath away
and hold it, breathing, in your mouth: each day
a fresh kill. I never know what you think.
We're old flames stalking each other — big game
purring repletion, sucking out marrow.
What seems a cry could be a cried-out name.
You dive. Sea-glints waver like a shuffled Tarot
till you surface, doing the butterfly: the same
quick-strung armspan loosing arrow after arrow.

Four ton of whimsy. Though the eye in its crow's-nest
of wrinkles is friendly, the trunk's salutation
unsettles the onlookers: three ghosts dressed
in feints of chalk. Their robes might be Asian;
their faces are faceless; and there I am
among them, anonymous to myself,
self-doubting, an unfilled outline, a clam —
true by indirection, faithful by stealth.
Beware of unwise men bearing gifts (guilt,
indifference and hurt): beware of me.
We sift the sky for lost kingdoms. A silt
of stars hides the one star at apogee,
this mirage of a life like water spilled
in the star-grains of Sinai or Gobi.

Lapidary

His craft was strife
And his last laugh
This epitaph –
A wasted life

She is deathless
The bronzed tomboy
Whose modes of joy
Left him breathless

The Abridgement

Then the sky dropped out of itself, skittish as a leaf,
And I walked forward, into, and out of, my life.
(It seemed shorter than I remembered, smaller.)
A man approached. An ingratiator. A smiler.
'Lovely here, isn't it? Breathe that air! Ambrosia!'
Affability was stamped on his face like a seizure.
Irrelevance pin-pricked his eyes. I turned away,
Looking for my life, but it was gone. Where? Why?
Meadowland stretched ahead, empty and serene.
Something twittered. A feathered friend. A Siren.

> *It will not die. It will not die.*
> *You loved her. You love her.*
> *Under that sky. Under this sky.*
> *It will not die.*

I had to be higher. The one hill was ploughland.
Glutinous clay, harrowed and grasping, it was gleaned
Of everything but an aftermath of mud.
I levered myself free of each and every clod
But one. 'That's it! Swing those arms! See you at the top!'
His words faded. The wind was getting up.
Branches clattered: the stutter of arrows growing louder.
The dying sun lit pines pitched in battle order.
An oriflamme of foliage was spruce
Flaring into gold, into flame, then speech.

> *It can't be killed. You mustn't try.*
> *She loved you. She loves you.*
> *You can't kill love. It will not die.*
> *It will not die.*

My gaze swooped down the valley, as though sight—
Avid and avian – had to kill what it sought.
My life waited. Day trembled on its edge.
The wind was still. Chopping sounds – an axe or adze—
Floated up like smoke as the forest shimmered
Beneath me until, astonished and ashamed,
I saw, silhouetted by the sky's reds and blues,
My life. A tree. A skinny tree. Axe-blows
Split my heart. Sawdust filled my mouth. Then gall.
This shivering tree. This beautiful, gawky girl.

> *You mustn't cry. You mustn't cry.*
> *What was, will be again.*
> *Both of us know. Now we can die.*
> *It will not die.*

'Bit of a facer, eh? Not to worry. Have a gargle!'
He was tugging a bottle through the zip of his cagoule.
'That your life? Kiss it goodbye! Hanging on's morbid,
    ghoulish . . .'
He was going to go on. I kneed him in the goolies.
'Oooof!' I ran downhill, outpacing his farewell. 'Oooof . . .'
I ran blind, toward the last of my life.
Leaf-whips opened my face and it streamed blood and sap
Till I came to a clearing and at last I could stop.
The man there set down his axe and took out tinder.
He gathered me up: complete, raw, tender.

> *There is no end, no by and by.*
> *There is us. Together.*
> *It will not die. It will not die.*
> *It will not die.*

The Gap

It's H and I've O.D.'d —
   Intravenous, straight to the heart —
And here I am stumbling toward an ode,
   A paean in reverse, a hymn to hurt,
Here I am, weepy, wondering, writing
    Out of love, out of loss,
      Out of my one-track mind, its rails empty
And aimed at a future as unwitting
    As you are, now you're all but dead to me,
      Now you're with someone else.

That douce rainbow of olive and tan, white and black
   Is the clothes you buy at The Gap
I see now, minus the labels at waist and neck
   You would remove by a surgical rip
With that de-stitching tool straight out of Bosch,
    Fanged steel ensuring skin was kissed
      By nothing but Cotton, 100%.
My wallet saved one label (a cheque never cashed)
    Till the day it gets binned: when I'm absent-
      Minded with loss, or brave, or rash.

Your white jeans had a workman's loop, handy for a hammer,
   Which, climbing into a cab ('Chinatown . . .'),
Snagged, and the seam gave, and gave me more:
   A private road to Paradise which, serpentine,
I took, exploring this gap, this fissure
    For my fingers, for the aficionado
      I am of you: your skin, your yawn, your laugh,
Your fugues of boredom, your sharpening into desire —
    While I could be wondering whether we'd make love,
      You'd want to fuck without further ado.

Soup for starters, four smoky bowls of hot-and-sour —
    Kim's choice – and this out-of-sync match, this pact
Of opposites, recalls the face I've seen Kim wear
    Listening to poetry, the face I call Baffled Respect.
So we ate and talked. And it was clear that Angela,
    Kim's wife, was not your type (and you weren't hers).
        China spoons chinked on china bowls.
You didn't like what she did to him: 'She defers.'
    I like, and dislike, how your heart rebels
        At conciliation: how it's spiky, cold, angular.

But I fret whether not having a heart to give
    Means not having a heart, Helen, at all.
(Is this hurt, putting on airs? Or love?
    Or my usual knack for being fatal?)
I fret about what's not there – my face has the gape
    Of the opening door pushed at too late
        As we collect all that is lost and last
And walk into that space where the ribs hug a gap
    The size of a fist, and inside that fist
        Random stars wait, infinite and unlit.

Notes

1. He suffered badly from landsickness.

2. She was a gladiator, straddling him, waiting for the thumbs down.

3. One of their main topics of conversation was their lack of topics of conversation.

4. That the word 'exergue' should exist!

5. Approached rationally, poetry has as much to recommend it as a bad smell.

6. She was a twin, the second-born. The first-born did the work; she emerged flawless.

7. As a child she insisted on having black dolls.

8. Absence makes the prick grow.

9. Loved, but not liked.

10. The clocks having gone back in the night, that morning he masturbated twice.

11. Stesichorus (632–556 BC) went blind after defaming Helen in a poem about the Trojan War. This has not survived, and only a fragment remains of the 'Palinode' (or poem of recantation) which won him back his sight.

12. A chalked sign outside a London hardware shop: Twinned with Galeries Lafayette.

13. He thought life was one long taxi ride.

14. Louis XIV was crowned in 1643. The sum of the figures of this date is 14. Ditto for the date of his death, 1715, and the number of years he reigned, 77. He was born in 1638. 1638 plus 1715 equals 3353.

15. After avoiding her for some years, he met her again by chance ('O' stalls in the Royal Albert Hall). Some weeks later, on November 14th, they met by design.

16. Fate is a random number of coincidences.

17. Did not all his uncertainties about her stem from an underlying uncertainty about himself?

18. Fulham Road. The number 14 bus to The Green Man.

19. He saw the dirty window, not the view.

20. Can you trust the heart? Can you trust the milometer on a used car?

21. He woke from a dream in which he was writing an elegy. One line ended with the word 'notwithstanding...'

22. The bulldozer is the size of Paddington Station, which it demolished this morning. It is now reducing the Albert Hall to rubble (wider still and wider). This first swathe through London will be 28 miles long. A second, of 14 miles, will be cut from the mid-point of the first, at an angle of 90°, out through Greenwich. The third and final swathe, of 28 miles, will be parallel to the first. After trenching, the whole figure will be filled with fuel. At dusk on January 4th, this will be set alight, burning till dawn on the 5th.

23. He said he didn't trust her. She said he was pathologically honest.

24. He called her by any number of names and compared her to any number of things (animal, fruit and mineral). He also said she was fourteen. With long red hair. And French. (No. No. *Non*.)

25. She was French with long red hair. Returning to her flat (in the *quatorzième*), their taxi waits as shoppers cross

the road. Golden letters on a department store window: *Jumelées avec Tracken's Hardware.*

26. A poem is a random number of coincidences.

27. Fate is a necessary number of coincidences.

28. Never to be called father. Never to be called mother.

29. 'Chanson' appeared in Ronsard's *Sonnets pour Hélène* (1578). A useful caveat on the truthfulness of love poetry was made by a disciple of Ronsard's, Amadis Jamyn: 'Aveugles sont les Amoureux/ Et souvent les Poètes mentent:/ Ne croyez donq tout ce que chantent/ Les hommes qui sont tous les deux.'

30. She was a day older than him.

31. He did not worship the ground she walked on. He worshipped her feet.

32. To take just one, the one with the mole above the heel: not, necessarily, beautiful in itself (though very soft and sexually active), it is beautiful in the way it is so thoroughly and sturdily itself. It can stand for the whole woman: completely incapable of self-doubt.

33. Making love, he'd tell her to look at him: her eyes were large, beautiful, sardonic.

34. The shortest distance between two people is a bed.

35. How much of his unhappiness was caused by her having left him, how much by him being left with himself?

36. At 20, love. At 30, pity. At 40, contempt. At 50, love again. So long a journey to return to the same place!

37. Thought outlasts feeling.

38. Before stepping out of the bath, she would carefully knock each foot against the side.

39. Before stepping out of the bath, she would carefully knock each foot against the side.

40. Feeling outlasts thought.

41. The Head of Light Entertainment is driven home to his Light Life.

42. Her assassin's walk at night, silent but for her neck-chain's whisper of silver, the only thing she was wearing as she came to bed, him lying there, happier than he knew.

43. Silver sounds gladder than gold.

44. The word and what it denotes meet on a narrow pavement: which one steps into the gutter?

45. They baffled each other: the attraction of incomprehensibles.

46. The conception, gestation and birth of nothing.

47. In her luxurious bed – the duck down, the 100% cotton, the white-on-white – she'd wake early and worry.

48. Her heart was pragmatic.

49. Loving is aces, liking is trumps.

50. They could only talk about their feelings by using metaphor and periphrasis. He thought of the GDR after the building of the Berlin Wall when the word 'wall' was virtually forbidden: one was to speak of 'the border' or 'the antifascist protective rampart...'

51. You are sentenced to life: your life.

52. A sonnet is the egg of a featherless bird.

53. Happily, he could no more leave her than fly. Unhappily, he was now avoiding her.

54. A life lived in retrospect, you and your past like the hunchback and his hump.

55. Unhappily, he could no more leave her than fly. Happily, he was now avoiding her.

56. Gratitude flowers between the paving stones.

The years left them ashamed,
Sharing their double shame:
Both wanting to be claimed
And both too weak to claim.

Morgenstern's Knee

A knee leads a solitary life.
It is a knee, just so!
It's not a bush! It's not a knife!
It is a knee, just so.

Once, in battle, a man
was blown to kingdom come.
The knee alone survived – as if
in a ciborium.

Which explains its solitary life.
It is a knee, just so.
It's not a bush, it's not a knife.
It is a knee, just so.

Gautier's Art

True form's refractory
And waits in stone or word:
  Glory
In subduing what's hard.

Mere constraint's not enough.
Brando's Method mutter
  Sounds gruff
Laced in pentameter,

But he grips the back-rows
When stumbling on splendour
  In prose:
'I coulda been a contender...'

Form is what's overcome.
Stone speaks clearer than clay.
  A thumb
Marks the potter's off-day.

Fight the mutual fight
With rock: be Parian,
  Pure, white;
Hew the empyrean.

Struck, the die-engraver's
Metal does not shiver,
  Lava's
Heat coined in cold silver.

When Apollo's eyes trace
A chalcedonic vein,
   The face
In the stone is divine.

No acrylics or oils.
Colours are fixed, not faked—
   Jewels
The enameller has baked.

Creation must be fired
By detail, your dogdays
   Inspired
By a heraldic blaze.

Carve the pomegranate
As fruit and fate: Mary's
   Granite
Passion never varies.

Life dies. Only symbols
Can preserve today's joy,
   Obols
And odes surface from Troy.

First planting in polder;
Marble clangs the ploughshare:
   Boulder
Or buried emperor?

The pale gods fade away,
But Homer's arias
   Will stay
Solid as bronze or brass.

So chisel, file and ream,
Striving with the hewn block:
    The dream
Emerges out of rock.

A Piece of Him
for Stephen Knight

A viaduct pub shoe-
horned under Waterloo,
The Hole in the Wall
is a wold: Sussex Ale
ploughs its furrow
like there's no tomorrow.
'Duw, I needed that!'
A navvy in a hard-hat
lowers a glass
laced with the lees
and flecks of thirst,
hops and their ghost
dry as the barman's grin.
'Same again?' 'Same again.'

A train thumps overhead.
I swallow and the dead,
without any fuss,
are with us.
I'd been sure as Pilate,
trusting to my palate
(What I've drunk, I've drunk),
till that *thunkety-thunk*
poured limbo in my ear.
What I hear isn't here.
Barrels crowding a chute,
a muffled shout,
or curse, or claim.
A ghost calling a name
on pain of death:
'Amleth ... Amleth ...'

[48]

And I was back,
a pint of Dark
then one of S.A.,
savouring the way
he span his tale,
nursing the ginger ale
he never sipped once
in an hour, the prince.
Hitting a storm,
leaving his farm,
he'd driven fast
through Bell Forest
('Like the clappers—
passed some coppers...')
to get here for midday:
the snug of The Old A
on Golate and 12th.
I drank his good health.
He settled in his seat
and adjusted his suit
(a two-piece from Sable):
his usual foible
of seeing it set off
by Niagaras of cuff.
I asked him straight out:
'Is Ffion all right?'
'Don't you know? Bugger me.
Flat Holm ... The nunnery.
I meant it as a joke.
A nun! Don't make me boak.
She'd be better off dead—
like her prick of a dad.'

With his Zeiss and thermos,
his slub-silk pyjamas
(the royal monogram
stitched in Ogham),
my Lord of the Gower
sits in his tall tower
scanning the Channel
out past the tunnel
where his pioners dig.
Gas-waste flares on a rig.
Flat Holm and Steep Holm
pacify the spume
as their bells toll
and the marker buoys roll,
sink, then start to rise.
A gull cries and cries.

He's one of the Taffia—
closer-knit than raffia—
he got it from Moelwyn
who's well in with Mostyn
who heard it from Nerys
who's (you know) with Carys
who's doing some sewing
for Cycle Clips Owen
who got it from Nia
off Iphegenia—
I'm not jesting—
who's like this with Iestyn
who got it from Dewi
who's indebted to me—
diolch to the Taffia
closer-knit than raffia.

I got the gen
on the old man
over a bacon roll,
crisp and surreal
prolepsis on a plate.
I'd lost the plot –
like the tea-stall sign
(that had to be seen,
disbelieved, ignored
or taken on board
in that state of grace
beyond common sense)
offering, with the Battenberg,
salt wit from Wittenberg
(or Splott): *We put the T
in Cardiff.* 'QED,'
as my Lord said,
cutting his bread.

'In the bedroom with Mam
I got a whiff of spam,
a gust of guano –
mano-a-mano
with her all day
then that pong of decay
outstinking the bed-pan:
the reek of an old man
humped in the bedding . . .
It did my head in.
When I took him outside
he begged and cried,
he shat and he pissed
and howled "Iesu Grist"
like a regular monk.
I diced him, chunk by chunk,

till I could hardly stand.
Duw, but I'm a dab hand
with the chopper!
The four-gallon copper
boiled him to bones and lard.
We tipped him in the yard.
When the goons came
eager for blame
and a patsy,
I played crazy:
"He's by the midden
feeding the mochyn!"
Then I was acting twp.
Now I can't cowing stop.'

The rest is ellipsis
dot dot dots of Ss
triple dashes of Os
the styptic prose
spoken by the dead
as he sleeps in bed
his kingdoms of kelp
not the slightest help
when St Elmo's fire
walks high on the tower
and wind screams
through his dreams
Mors
out of the Bahamas
a cargo of timbers
shifting in a Force 10
twenty-six men
The Oak

First light's withheld
as Prime is belled –
solus – and cormorants
enter the dance
of wave on wave,
black-feathered, grave.
Waiting for dawn
on the nunnery lawn,
one of The Natterjacks
of Gabalfa (PLATE X:
Bufo calamita)
hymns in hexameter
the flora of Flat Holm,
the brine, the loam!
A sister in her cell
wakes to the bell
and lies in the gloom
of a Christian room
in this nunnery
on the sea
flat as a mirror,
flat as a mirror.

Disclaimer

Certain words may offend certain sensibilities.

    cig (meat)   hiraeth (homesickness)
    diolch (thank you)   mochyn (pig)
    Duw (God)   twp (foolish)

Redress, however, is unlikely.

The murdered counsellor can be found in Saxo Grammaticus. A later writer omitted his being fed to swine and gave him two names, Carambis (derived from *Crambe bis posita mors est*: Cabbage served twice is death) and Polonius.

Splott and Gabalfa are parts of Cardiff. Golate is a street there and The Old A a pub. Another of its pubs, The Oak, has no connection with the ship of that name, the last to send an SOS in Morse.

Mr C. Owen of Monmouth would like it known that he does not ride, nor has he ever ridden, a bicycle.